DEVOTIONS

of our Lord

DEVOTIONS

OF OUR LORD

By: Kurtis M. Williams,
Maralee G. Williams and Holly M.
Williams.

"Reading this book may keep you from sin."

"SIN MAY KEEP YOU FROM READING THIS BOOK".

CONTENTS

ART PRINTS AVAILABLE FOR SALE INDIVIDUALLY OR AS A SET

The paintings, drawings, and pictorial representations—from the cover to scripture depictions—created by Kurtis M. Williams are available for purchase individually or as a set. Each print is priced at $10.00, plus shipping and handling at $6.00 for individual purchases. A complete set of all the prints in this collection is available for $120.00, which includes postage and handling.

To order, please contact:
Email: kurtiswilliams@myyahoo.com
Phone: Maralee Grace Williams, Director of Marketing: 815-558-4991

A NOTE FROM THE AUTHOR & ARTIST

These paintings and drawings were completed over a nine-year period of personal struggles while I was in prison and as I came to know the Lord through His holy word. Every brushstroke and depiction was a living testament to how God's grace works within me, my family, and the people He brings into our lives.

I hope that readers, too, will find themselves drawn closer to God in their daily devotions. May God bless each and every one of you.

The proceeds from this book will support the creation of further works by the author and artist.

ABOUT THE AUTHORS

Kurtis M. Williams was baptized on January 24, 1998, at Joliet Correctional Center after seeing his beautiful daughter, Holly Michelle Williams. He has since dedicated his life and soul to the Lord and his family. Kurtis has written several books, but it was through the trials of prison, separation from his family, and fellowship with his cousins that he learned how the Lord defines His purpose in all of us.

Maralee Grace Williams, a cancer survivor and mother to Holly Michelle Williams, is a prolific gardener who loves fishing, cooking, and serving God's will with her generous heart. She ends all her greetings and conversations with, "God bless you," accompanied by a smile that brightens any room.

Holly Michelle Williams is a beautiful model and influencer. She and her mother, Maralee Grace Williams, were both baptized on April 30, 2024. Holly has dedicated her life to God, her family, and her pursuit of God's purpose through her work and fellowship. She is also certified in commercial makeup, hair, and cosmetology.

As a family, we have inspired one another to create this 52-week devotional to share the inspiration, hope, and purpose that God has given us.

God bless all the readers who enjoy Kurtis' paintings depicted in this book. We thank the Lord for His guidance.

DEDICATION

Kurtis M. Williams, Holly Michelle Williams, and Maralee G. Williams would like to dedicate this book to the Lord Jesus Christ and Mr. Kerry D. Knodle, as well as Darcy and John Hoffman, Brittany and Dalton Epperly, Brielle and Patrick Crouse, Paige and Zach, and all our combined families. We thank you for allowing us to seek out God's purpose in health, spirit, and through our daily life struggles.

May the Lord bless each and every one of you in all regards.

PART 1

UNDER HIS WINGS

"In the shadow of thy wings will I make my refuge."
—Psalm 57.

Could anything be more tenderly gracious than this figure hiding under the shadow of God's wings? It speaks of bosom-warmth, and bosom-shelter, and bosom-rest. "Let me do thy bosom fly!"

And what strong wings they are! Under those wings, I am secure even from the lions. My animal passions shall not hurt me when I am "Hiding in God."

The fiercest onslaughts of the devil are powerless to break those mighty wings. The tenderest little chick, "one of these little ones", nestling behind this soft and gentle shelter, shall be perfectly secure; "none of its bones shall be broken".

I do not wonder that this sheltering psalmist begins to sing! "I will sing and give praise!" I have often listened to the sheltering chicks, hiding behind the mother's wings, and I have heard that quaint, comfortable, contented sound for which our language has no name. It is a sound of incipient song, the musical murmur of satisfaction. "I will sing unto thee...for thy mercy is great".

THE SOUL IN PRISON

"Bring my soul out of prison!" —Psalm 142.

I, Too have my prison-house, and only the Lord can deliver me. There is a prison of brick and mortar and there is also a prison of sin. It is a dark and suffocating hole, without friendly light or morning air. And it is haunted by affrighting shapes, as though my iniquities had incarnated themselves in ugly and repulsive forms. None can but the Lord can bring me out from this place!

There is also a prison-place of sorrow. My griefs sometimes wrap me about like cold confining walls, which have neither windows nor doors. It seems as though a fluid sorrow can congeal into a cold, hard temperment, and hold me in its icy embrace. And... none but the Lord can bring me out from this place!

And there is a prison of death. I must perforce pass through the gate of death. Shall I find it a castle of gloom, or is there another gate through which I shall emerge into the fair, sweet paradise of God? My master is Lord of the road! And he tells me that death shall not be a castle of captivity, but only a thoroughfare through which I shall pass into the realm of eternal day within His kingdom.

HOW TO APPROACH A CRISIS

"It shall be given you in That same hour..."
—Matthew 10:16-28

And so I am not to worry about the coming crisis! "God never is before His time, and never is behind!" When the hour is come, I shall find that the great Host hath made "all things ready."

When the crisis comes He will tell me how to rest. It is a great matter to know just how to rest—how to be quiet when "all without tumultuous seems." We irritate and excite our souls about the coming emergency, and we approach it with worn and feverish spirits, and so mark our Master's purpose and work.

When the crisis comes He will tell me what to do. The orders are not given until the appointed day. Why should I fume and fret and worry as to what the sealed envelope contains? "It is enough that He knows all." And when the hour strikes the secrets shall be revealed. And when the crisis comes He will tell me what to say. I need not begin to prepare my retorts and my responses. What shall I say when death comes? To me or my loved ones? Never mind, He will tell thee. And what when sorrow or persecution comes? Never mind, He will tell thee.

TRANSFORMING THE HARD HEART

"The Lord turned the flint into a fountain of waters."
—Psalm 114.

What violent conjunction, the flint becoming the birthplace of a spring! And yet this is happening every day. Men and women who are hard as the flint, "whose hearts are like the nether millstone," become springs of gentleness and fountains of exquisite compassion.

Beautiful graces, like lovely ferns, grow in the home of severities and transform the grim, stern soul into a garden of fragrant friendships. This is what Zacchaeus was like when his flint became a fountain. It is when Matthew the publican was like when the Lord changed his hard heart into a land of springs.

No one is "too far gone". No hardness is beyond the love and pity of God. The well of eternal life can gush forth even in a desert of waste, and "where sin abounds grace doth much more abound". Let us bring our hardness to the Lord. Let us see what he can make of our flint. When we are dry and "feelingless", and desire is dead, let us bring the Sahara to the great Restorer, and "the blossom like the rose".

SPIRITUAL BUOYANCY

"When thou passeth through the waters they shall not overflow thee"
—Isaiah 43:1-7.

When Mrs. Booth, The Mother of the Salvation Army was dying, she quietly said; "The waters are rising but I am not sinking".

Often she had been saying that all throughout her life. Other floods besides the waters of death had gathered about her soul. Often had the floods been out and the roads were deep in affliction, but she had never sunk! The good Lord made her buoyant, and she rode upon the storm!

This, then, is the promise of the Lord, not that the waters of trouble shall never...gather about the believer, but that he or she shall never be overwhelmed. He or she shall keep his or her head above them. Yes, to him or her shall be given the grace of aboveness. He or she shall never be under, always above! It is the precious gift of spiritual buoyancy, sanctified good spirits, the power of the Christian hope. When we are in Christ Jesus circumstances shall never be our master. One is our Master, and "we are more than conquerors in Him that Loved us, and washed us from our sins in His own blood."

THE HOME-BIRD

Psalm 91.

I read a sentence the other day in which a very powerful modern writer describes a certain woman as "having God on her visiting list". We may recoil from a phrase, such as this, but it's vital and describes a very awful commonplace. Countless millions have God on their visiting list. They pay Him courtesy calls, and between the calls He is forgotten. Perhaps the call is paid once a week in the social functions of worship. Perhaps it is paid more rarely, like calls between comparative strangers. How great the contrast between a caller and one who dwells in the secret place! It is the difference between one who flits about on a score of fancies and one who settles down in the solid satisfaction of a supreme affection.

"Shall abide under the shadow of the Almighty!" Such is the reward of the "home-bird," "the settled friend of the Lord". The shadow of the Lord shall rest upon Him and her continually. I sometimes read of our politicians being "shadowed" by protective police.

In an infinitely more real and intimate sense of the soul that dwells in "the secret place" is shadowed by the sleepless grace and love of Jesus Christ, our Lord and Savior.

NOT THESE THINGS WITHOUT FAITH

Hebrews 11:1-7.

Not the setbacks
but the lessons.

Not the excuses,
but the truth.

Not the destination
but the journey.

Not the age
But the wisdom.

Not the accomplishments,
but the goal.

Not the time spent,
but the love.

Not the sorrow,
but the joy.

Not the doubt,
but the hope.

Not what you do,
but who you are in your faith.

CLEAN AND UNCLEAN ANGER

Ephesians 4:25-32

"Let all anger be put away from you!" The apostle Paul wrote the words. "Be angry but do not sin". My power of anger is not to be destroyed, it is to be transformed and purified.

Anger can be an unclean bonfire; it can be like "a sea of glass mingled with fire!" There can be more smoke than light in it, more selfishness and more selfish passion than holy purpose. The fuel that feeds it may be envy, and jealousy, and spite, and not a big desire for the good of men or women and the glory of God. Worldly anger "is set on fire of hell"; Holy anger borrows flame from the alter-fires of God.

Our anger reveals our character. What is the quality of our anger? What kindles it? Is it incited by our own wrongs, or by the wrongs of another? Is it set on fire by self-indulgence? or by a noble sympathy? Here is a sentence which describes the anger of the Apostle Paul: "Who is made to stumble and I burn not?" Paul's anger was made to burn by oppression, by the cruelty inflicted upon his fellow men. His fire had nothing unclean in it; it was pure as the flame of oxygen.

This is the anger we must cherish. We cannot "work ourselves up" into it. We must seek to be "baptized with the Holy Ghost and with fire".

THE WITNESS OF YESTERDAY

Psalm 78:1-8

Our yesterdays are to be teachers of our children. We are to take them over our road and show them the pitfalls where we stumbled and where the snares were that lured us away. And we are to show them how we found the springs of grace, and how the Lord made Himself known to us in daily providence and care. We are to relate his exploits, "His wonderous and wonderful dealings with the children of men". We must make our life witness of God to our children, and when their minds roam over our road they must see it radiantly with the grace and mercy offered by the Lord.

The best inheritance I can give my child is a steadfast witness of my knowledge and wisdom led by God's grace and the wisdom of His promises. The testimony of a light that never failed may give our children the needful wisdom when their own way becomes troubled with clouds of darkness. And what a story it is, this story of deeds of our gracious God. It is full of quickening for weary and desponding souls. It is a perfect reservoir of inspiration for those whose desire has failed, and in whose lives the wells of impulse to strive have become dry. Let us bring forward yesterday's wealth to enrich the life of today. "Do ye not remember the miracle of the loaves?"

IN A CELLAR OF AFFLICTION

Psalm 34:9-22.

Samuel Rutherford used to say that whenever he found himself in the cellars of afflictions he used to look about for the King's wine. He would look for the wine bottles of the promises and drink rich draughts of vitalizing grace. And surely that is the best deliverance in all affliction, to be made so spiritually exhilarant that we can rise above it. I might be taken out of affliction, and emerge a poor slave and weakling. I might remain in affliction, and yet be king in the seeming servitude, "more than conqueror" in Christ Jesus. It is the greater thing to have a "table prepared before me in the presence of mine enemies". It is good to be able to sing in the sunny noonday: It is better still to be able to sing songs in the night as well.

And the deliverance may always be ours in Christ Jesus. The Lord may not smooth out our circumstances, but we may have the real right of peace. He may not save us from the sorrows of a newly cut grave, but we may have the glorious strength of the immortal hope.

God will enable us to be masters of all our circumstances, and none shall have a deadly hold upon us.

THE PROCESS PATIENCE

"Ye have seen the end of the Lord:
That the Lord is very pitiful, and of tender mercy".
—James 5:7-11.

And we are bidden to be patient. "We must wait to the end of the Lord." The Lord's ends are attained through very mysterious means. Sometimes the means are in contrast to the ends. He works toward the harvest through winter's frost and snow. The maker of chaste and delicate porcelain reaches his lovely ends through an awful mortar, where the raw material of bone and clay is pounded into a cream. In that mortar-chamber, we have no hint of the finished ware. But be patient, even in this chamber of affliction the ware is on the way to glory!

And so it is with the ministries of our Lord. He leads us through discords into harmonies, through opposition into union, through adversities into peace. His means of grace are "processes", sometimes gentle, sometimes severe; and our folly is to assume that we have reached His ends when we are only on the way to them. "The end of the Lord is very pitiful and of tender mercy". "Be patient therefore", until it shall be spoken of thee and me, "And God saw that it was good".

THE THREE GARDENS

Revelation 22:1-14.

The Bible opens with a garden. It closes with a garden. The first is the Paradise that is lost. The last is Paradise regained. And between the two there is a third garden of Gethsemane. And it is through the unspeakable bitterness and desolation of Gethsemane that we find again the glorious garden through which flows "the river of water of life". Without Gethsemane no New Jerusalem! Without its mysterious and unfathomable night, no blessed sunrise of eternal hope! "We were reconciled to God by the death of His son."

We are always in dire peril of regarding our redemption lightly. We hold it cheaply. Privileges easily come to be esteemed as rights. And even grace itself can lose the strength of heavenly favor and can be received and used as our due. "Gethsemane can I forget?" Yes, I can; and in the forgetfulness, I lose the sacred awe of my redemption, and I miss the real glory of "Paradise regained."

"Ye are not your own; ye are bought with a price." That is the remembrance that keeps the spirit lowly, and that fills the heart with love for Him "whose I am," and whom I ought to serve.

CROWDING OUT GOD

"Lest thou Forget."
—Deuteronomy 4:5-13.

That is surely the worst affront we can put upon anybody. We may oppose a man and hinder him in his work, or we may directly injure him, or we may directly injure him, and treat him as nothing. Or we may forget him! Opposition, injury, contempt, neglect, forgetfulness! Surely this is a descending scale, and the last is the worst. And yet we can forget the Lord God. We can easily put Him out of our minds. We can live as though He were dead. "My children have forgotten me".

What shall we do to escape this great disaster? "Take heed to thyself". To take heed is to be at the helm and not asleep within thy home. It is to steer and not to drift. It is to keep our eyes on the compass and our hands on the wheel. It is to know where we are going. We never deliberately forget our Lord; we carelessly drift into it. "Take heed".

"And keep thy soul diligently." Gardens run to seed, and ill weeds grow everywhere. The fair things are crowded out, and the weed reigns havoc. It is ever so with my soul. If I neglect it, the seeds that flower my holy desire to devotion will be choked by weeds of worldliness! God will be crowded out, and the garden of the soul will become a wilderness of neglect and sin.

SERENITY IN THE TEMPEST

Job 19:23-27.

Perhaps I am akin to Job in having experienced the pressure of calamity. I have felt the shock of adverse circumstances, and the house of my life has trembled in the convulsion. Or death has been at my door and has returned again and again, and every time it has left me weeping! All God's billows have gone over me! Thus, verily, I can take my place by the patriarch Job.

Thus, I can share his witness, "I know that my redeemer liveth"? Have I a calm assurance that my ruler is not caprice? When death knocked at my door, did I know that the King had sent him? When some cherished scheme toppled into ruin, had I any thought that the Lord's hand was concerned in the "shaking"? Even when my circumstances are dubious, and I cannot trace a gracious purpose, do I know that my vindicator liveth, and that someday he will justify all happenings on and within the troubled road?

I will pay for this gracious confidence. I would have a firm step even among disappointments; yeah, I would "sing songs in the night!"

BLESSINGS AND CURSINGS

"He read all the words of the law, the blessings and cursings."
—Joshua 8:30-35.

We are inclined to only read what pleases us, to hug the blessings and ignore the warnings. We bask in the light, we close our eyes to the lightning. We recount the promises, we shut our ears to the rebukes. We love the passages which speak of our Lord's gentleness, we turn away from those which reveal his severity. And all this is unwise, and therefore unhealthy. We become spiritually soft and anemic. We lack moral stamina. We are incapable of noble hatred and of holy scorn. We are invertebrates, and on the evil day, we are not able to stand.

We must read "all the words of the law, the blessings and the cursings." We must let the Lord brace us with His severities. We must gaze steadily upon the appalling fearfulness of sin, and upon its terrific issues. At all costs, we must get rid of the spurious gentleness that holds compromise with uncleanness, that effeminate affection which is destitute of holy fire! We must seek the Love which burns everlasting against all sin; we must seek the gentleness which can fiercely grip a poisonous growth and tear it out to its last hidden root! We must seek that holy love which is as a "Consuming fire."

REGISTERING A VERDICT

"The Lord our God we will serve, and his voice will we obey."
—Joshua 24:22-28

Here was a definite decision. Our peril is that we spend our life in wavering and we never decide. We are like a jury which is always hearing evidence and never gives a verdict. We do much thinking, but we never make up our minds. We let our eyes wander over many things, But we make no choices. Life has no crisis, no culmination.

Now people who never decide spend their days in hoping to do so. But this kind of life becomes a vagrancy and not a noble and illuminated crusade. We drift through our days, we do not steer, and we never arrive at any rich and stately haven.

It is therefore vitally wise to "make a vow unto the Lord."

It is good to pull our loose thinking together to "gird up the loins of the mind". Let a man, at some definite place, and at some definite moment, make the supreme choice of his life.

THE BULB AND THE SOIL

"He that hath my commandments, and keepeth them, He it is that Loveth me..."
—John 14:15-24.

Yes; but how can I keep them? Someone sent a bulb which requires a certain kind of soil, but he also sent me the soil in which to grow it. He sent instructions, but he also sent power. And when I am bidden to keep a commandment I feel as though I have received the bulb but not the soil! But is this God's way of dealing with His people? I will read on if perchance I may find the gift of the soil.

"He that abideth in me... The same bringeth forth much fruit." That is the gift I seek. For the keeping of His commandments, The Lord provides Himself. I am not called upon to raise fruits out of the soil of my own will, Out of my own infirmity as aspiration or desire. I can rest everything in God! I can "abide in Him." And I may have the Holy energies of the God Head to produce in me the fruits of a Holy and obedient life.

The good Lord provides both the bulb and the soil. It is the tragedy of life that we forget this, and seek to make a soil bed of our own, And thus do we suffer the calamity of fruitless labor, the heavy drudgery of tasks beyond our strength. "Come unto me, all ye that labor and are heavy laden, and I will give you rest."

GRUDGES

"Thou shalt not bear any grudge."
—Leviticus 19:11-18.

How searching is that demand upon the soul! By forgiveness of my brother or sister is to be complete. Sullenness is to remain, no sulky temper which so easily gives birth to thunder and lightning. There is to be no painful aloofness, no assumption of a superiority which rains contempt upon the offender. When I forgive, I am not to carry any powder forward on the journey. I am to empty out all my explosives, all my ammunition of anger and revenge. I am not to "bear any grudge".

I cannot meet this demand. It is altogether beyond me. I might utter words of forgiveness, but I cannot reveal a clear, bright, blue sky without a touch storm brewing anywhere. But the Lord of Grace can do it for me. He can change my weather. He can create a new climate. He can "renew a right spirit within me", and in that Holy atmosphere, nothing shall live which seeks to poison and destroy. Grudges shall die "like cloud spots in the dawn." Revenge, that awful creation of the unclean, feverish soul, shall give place to goodwill, the strong genial presence which makes it home in the new heart.

BIBLE SCRIPTURE SUDOKU

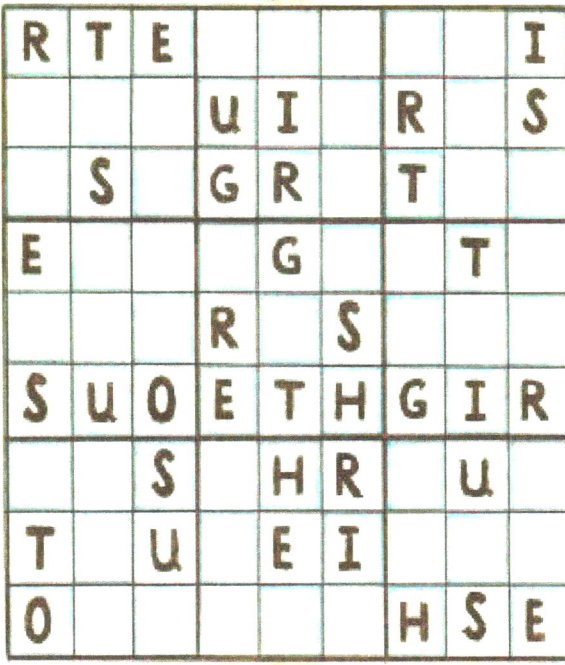

R	T	E						I
			U	I	R		R	S
	S		G	R		T		
E				G			T	
		R		S				
S	U	O	E	T	H	G	I	R
	S		H	R		U		
T	U		E	I				
O					H	S	E	

TRIVIA
WORD SEARCH

TWO WAYS OF LIFE

Matthew 7:13-29

"Enter the Narrow gate, For the wide gate is the way that leads to destruction", "and that there are many who go by it". My life has had many opportunities to understand through trials of choices and consequences to those decisions related to those choices what avails itself. Here Jesus tells us in certain terms of the various contrasts between trees and fruits and groups of peoples as representations of who and what we choose by our will to associate ourselves with that either leads to the Kingdom of God or destruction through an eternity in hell.

Not just who... we choose to associate ourselves with but in the literal sense of what we consume into our bodies., The temple of God while we walk in His grace.

A good representation today is for us to say what we mean and mean what we say when we pray and ask God for guidance in our walk in His Grace. Jesus wants to be part of everything in our lives, when we act according to the world and the temptations that dissuade us from the Kingdom, through worldly pleasures that are outside family and kingdom rich soil, we lead ourselves into the valley of the shadow of death and destruction! Lead me Lord today down and up the path of Life that allows me to serve you and leads me and who I fellowship with to the fruits of your kingdom of Life!

COUNSEL AND MIGHT

Psalm 119:33-40.

The psalmist prays for and illuminated understanding. "Teach me, O Lord, the way of thy statutes." We are so prone to be children of the twilight, and to see things out of their true proportions. Therefore do we need to be daily taught? I must go into the School of the Lord, and in docility of spirit, I must sit at His feet. "O, teach me, Lord, teach even me!"

And the psalmist prays for rectified inclinations. "Incline my heart unto thy testimonies." We so often have the wrong bias, the fatal taste, and our desires are all against the will of the Lord. If only my leanings were toward the Lord, how swift my progress would be! I strive to walk after holiness; while my inclinations are in the realm of sin. And so, I need a clean mouth, with an appetite for only the beauty and the truth. "Blessed are they that hunger after righteousness."

And the Psalmist prays for a strenuous will. "Make me to go in the path of thy commandments." He is praying for "go", for moral persistence, for power to crash through all obstacles which may impede his heavenly progress. And such is my need. Good Lord, endow me with a will like "an iron pillar," and help me to "stand in the evil of this day."

THE DARK BETRAYAL

John 18:1-14.

Our Master, the Lord was betrayed by a disciple, "One of the twelve". The blow came from one of "His own household." The world employed a "friend" to execute its dark design. And so our intimacy with Christ may be our peril; our very association may be made our temptation. The devil would rather gain one belonging to the inner circle than a thousand who stand confessed as the friends of the world.

What am I doing in the Kingdom? Can I be trusted? Or am I in the pay of the evil one? And our Master was betrayed in the Garden of Prayer. In the most hallowed place, the betrayer gave the most unholy kiss. He brought his defilement into the most awe-inspiring sanctuary the world has ever known. And so may it be with me. I can kindle the unclean fire in the church. I can stab my Lord when I am on my knees. When I am in apparent devotion I can be in league with the powers of darkness.

And this darkness or "dark betrayal" was for money! The Lord of Glory was bartered for thirty pieces of silver! And the difference between Judas and many men is that they often sell their Lord for less! From the power of Mammon, and from the blindness which falls upon his victims, Good Lord, deliver me!

THE FEAR OF MAN

John 18:15-27.

And this disciple who had been surnamed "The Rock"! Our Lord looked into the future and He saw Simon's Character, compacted by grace and discipline into a texture tough and firm as granite. But there is not much granite here! Peter is yet loose and yielding; more like a bending reed than an unshakeable rock. A serving girl whispers, and his timid heart flings a lie to his lips and he denies his Lord.

Peter denied the Master, and not because he coveted money, but because he feared men. He was not seeking crowns, but escaping frowns. He was not clutching at the garland, but avoiding the sword. It was not avarice but cowardice which determined his ways. He shrank from crucifixion! He saw a possible cross, and with a great lie, he passed on the other side.

But the Lord has not done with Peter. He is still "in the making". Some day he will justify his new name. Some day we shall find it written: "When they saw the boldness of Peter, they Marveled! Once a maid could make him tremble. Now he can stand in high places, "steadfast and unmovable"!

From the spirit of cowardice and from all temporizing, and from the unholy fear of man, deliver me, Good Lord!

THE COMING OF THE LORD

Luke 17:22-32

In a certain way, the Lord is coming every moment. And the great art of Christian living is to be able to discern Him when He arrives and He may appear as the village carpenter, or we may "suppose Him to be one of the gardeners," and we mistake His appearing! He may meet us in some lowly duty, or in some seemingly unpleasant task, He may shine in the cheeriness of some triumph, or whisper to us in a message of good news. "I come again". And if our eyes are open we shall see Him coming continually. It is by this perception that the value of our life is measured and weighed.

But He will also come again "suddenly" when the soul will be translated into unknown climes. He will come again in the sable robes of death. Shall we know Him? Will our eyes be so keen and true that we shall be able to pierce the dark veil and say "It is the Lord!" This has been the joyful experience of countless multitudes. When the summons came their souls went forth, not as victims to encounter death, but as the bride "to meet the bridegroom!" They had intimacy with Him in life; they had glorious fellowship with Him in death!

EXALTATION BY SEPARATION

2 Corinthians 6:11-18

When we turn away from the world and leave it, we ourselves are not left to desolation and being alone. When we "come out from among them" the Lord receives us! He is waiting for us. The new companionship is ours the moment the old companionship is ended. "I will not leave you comfortless." What we have lost is compensated by infinite and eternal gain. We have lost "the whole world" and gained "the unsearchable riches of Christ."

And therefore separation is exaltation. We leave the muddy pleasures of Sodom and "we drink of the river of His pleasures." We leave "the garish day," and all the feverish life of Vanity Fair, and He maketh us to lie down in green pastures," He leadeth us beside the still waters". We leave transient sensation, we receive the bread of eternity. We forfeit fireworks, we gain the stars!

What fools we are, and blind! We prefer the scorched desert of Sodom to the Garden of Eden. We prefer a loud reputation to noble character. We prefer delirium to joy. We prefer human applause to the praise of God. We prefer a fading garland to the crown of the Lord, that we may receive our sight!

NEAR HOME

2 Timothy 4:1-8

Here is the most valiant pilgrim nearing home! By the mercy of Christ, he can look back upon a brave day, and there's a fine hopeful light in the evening sky.

He has fought well! "I have fought a good fight." And his has been a good field. The enemy has never regarded him as a leader in the army of the Lord and against him has the fiercest fight been waged. But he has never lost his Stained flag like our Nation.

And he will run well. "I have finished my course." There was no melancholy turning back when the feverish start had cooled. There was no shrinking when the biting wind of malice and persecution swept across his track. On and on he ran, with increasing speed and ardour, until he reached the goal.

And well had he guarded his treasure! "I have kept the faith." He was the custodian of unsearchable riches", and he watched day and night, lest an infernal burglar should despoil him with wealth.

He guarded his gospel, his liberty, his hope, as the sentinels guard the crown jewels in the tower.

And now the hard day is nearly over. "Henceforth there is laid up for me a crown of righteousness which the Lord will give me at that day."

THINGS MISSING IN HEAVEN

John 21:1-7.

What a number of "conspicuous absences" there are to be in "the homeland!" No more sea! John was in Patmos, and the sea rolled between him and his kinsmen. The sea was a minister of estrangement. But in the home country, every cause of separation is to be done away, and the family life is to be one of inconceivable intimacy. No more sea!

And no pain! Its work is done, and therefore the worker is put away. When the building is completed the scaffolding may be removed. When the patient is in good health medicine bottles can be dispensed with. And so shall it be with pain and all its attendants. "The inhabitant never says; 'I am sick!'"

And no more death! The last enemy that shall be destroyed is death". Yes, He, too, shall drop his scythe, and his lax hand shall destroy no more forever. Death himself shall die! And all things that have shared His work shall die with him. "The former things have passed away." The wedding peal which becomes the lamb's bride will ring the funeral knell of death and all his sable company.

PART 2

HOME LIFE IN GOD

John 17:20-26

The home-life in God is to be a life of perfect union—"I in them, and thou in me." Home is only another name for union. It is the perfect fusion of life with life, the harmonizing of differences as many different notes combined to form the mystery of choral song. And so will it be in the home-land! Our manifold individualities will be retained, but we shall "fit into one another," and in the perfect harmony we shall hear the "new song" of heaven.

And we are to prepare that union by the contemplation of the glory of the Lord. "That they may behold my glory." Yes, and we can begin to do that now.

We can lift our eyes away from the ugly compromises of men and fix them upon the radiant holiness of the Lord. We can look away from the dirty alpine village and gaze upon the virgin snow of the uplifted heights. "Looking unto Jesus!"

And in that contemplation we shall most assuredly become transformed. "I have given unto them the glory which thou gavest me." That is our wonderful possibility. For thee and me is this prize afforded, we can "live awake in his likeness."

THE GREAT COMPANION

John 14:15-31

And so even the road is to have the home-feeling in it. "I will not leave you orphans." Yes; there is to be something of home even in the way to it. I find something of Illinois even in Beloit, Wisconsin; Rockford, Illinois gives me a taste of Beloit. My Lord will not leave me comfortless. Heaven runs over, and I find its bounty before I arrive at its gates.

"The valley of Baca" becomes "a well." And there are to be wonderful provisions to speed the pilgrim's feet. "I will manifest myself unto him." At unexpected corners the glory breaks! We shall be assuming that we have picked up a common traveler, and suddenly we shall discover it is the Lord, for he will be made known to us "in the breaking of bread."

And at many "risings" of the road, where the climbing is stiff and burdensome, we shall be inspired with many a glorious view, and we shall see "the land that is very far off."

The one condition is, that I keep His word. If I am obedient, He will appear unto me, and the humdrum will shine with miracles of grace.

SICKNESS AMONG CHRIST'S FRIENDS

John 11:1-16

And sickness can enter the circle of friends of the Lord. "He whom lovest is sick." My sicknesses do not mean that I have lost his favour. The shadow is His, as well as the sunshine. When He removes me from the glare of boisterous health it may be because of some spiritual fern which needs ministry of the shade. "This sickness is... for the Glory of God." Something beautiful will spring out of the shadowed seclusion, something which shall spread abroad the name and fame of God.

And, therefore, I do not wonder at the Lord's delay. He did not hasten away to the sick friend: "He abode two days still in the same place where he was." Shall I put it like this: the awakening bulbs were not yet ready for the brighter light—just a little more shade! We are impatient to get healthy; the Lord desires that we become holy. Our physical sickness is continued in order that we may put on our spiritual strength.

And there are others besides sick Lazarus concerned in sickness: "I am glad for your sakes I was not there." The disciples were included in the divine scheme. Their spiritual welfare was to be affected by it. Let me ever remember that the circle affected by sickness is always wider than the patient's bed. And may God be glorified in all as they receive their blessings.

THE POWER OF THE CROSS

John 10:11-18

"Lay down my life." In that supreme sacrifice all other sacrifices turn pale. In the power of that sacrifice, the backest guilt finds forgiveness. Its energies seek out the ruined and desolate life with glorious offer of renewal. When the Lord laid down the entire race found new beginnings. Our hope is born at the Cross. It is there that "the burden of our sins rolls away". In His night we find daybreak. When He said, "It is finished", our soul could then sing, "life has begun".

And so, pilgrims gather at the Cross. Songs are heard there, the "sweetest ever sung by mortal tongues". And the power of the Cross never wanes. Its glorious grace reaches the soul today as in the earliest days. It inspires the despairing heart. It transforms the mind. It remakes the tissue of the will. There is no shattered power that the power of the Cross cannot restore. "We are complete in Him".

"In the Cross of Christ I have glory", towering over the wrecks of time; All the light of sacred story...Gathers round its head sublime".

OVERCHARGING THE HEART

Luke 21:25-36

Here is great peril. Our hearts may be "overcharged" with surfeiting, and drunkenness, and cares of this life, and so that day that comes upon you where your unaware. "Our mode of living may send spirits to sleep". Yes, we may so ill-use our bodies that the watchman sleeps his post! We can over-eat, and dim our moral sight. A man's daily meals have vital relationship with his vision of the Lord. If I would have a clear spirit I must not overburden the flesh.

And therefore I am bidden to "take heed" to myself. I must exercise common sense, the most important of all the senses. I must put a bridle upon my appetites, and hold it in subjection to our Lord. And I must watch! The devil is surpassingly cunning, and if he can, he will mix an opiate even within the sacramental wine. He will lure me among the winsome poppies, and put me into a perilous sleep.

And I must "Pray"! I have a great and glorious Defender! Let me humbly yet confidently use him, and I shall be delivered from the snares of appetites that are outside of our Lord, and from the benumbing influences of all excess.

INVINCIBLE RELIANCE

Hebrews 11:17-22.

Accounting that God was able. "That is the faith that makes moral heroes. That is the faith that prompts mighty ventures and crusades. It is faith in God's willingness and ability to redeem His promises and it is faith that I do my part while knowing that most assuredly he will do his. It is faith that he cannot possibly fail. It is faith that when He makes a promise, the money is already in the bank. It is faith that when He sends me into the wilderness the secret harvest is already ripe from which he will give me "daily bread". It is faith that "all things are now ready", and in that faith I will face the apparently impossible tasks.

And thus the "impossible" leads me to the "prepared". The desert leads me to "fields white already". The hard call to sacrifice leads me to the "lamb in the thicket". "God is able" and he is never behind the time. The critical need unveils His grace.

Faith goes out on this invincible reliance. It is "The assurance of things hoped for". And by faith it inherits these things and is rich and strong in their possession.

THE TEST OF FULLNESS

Deuteronomy 8:1-10

And thou shalt eat and be full, and thou shalt bless the Lord thy God. Fullness is surely a more searching test than want. Fullness induces sleep and forgetfulness. Many a man fights a good fight with Apollyon in the narrow way, who lapses into sleepy indifference on enchanted ground. Men often sit down to a full table without "grace". Pain cries out to God, while boisterous health strides along in heedlessness. Yes, it is our fullness that constitutes our direst peril. "This was the iniquity of Sodom, fullness of bread and abundance of idleness."

And so our tests may come on the sunny day. A nation's supreme tests may come in its prosperity. The sunshine may do more damage than the lightning. The soul may falter even in a great land where the "sun shines night and day".

Prayer must not, therefore, tarry until sickness and adversity come. We must "Pray without ceasing" in the cloudless noon, lest we are stricken with "the arrow that flieth by day". We must seek the eternal strength when no apparent enemy crouches at our gates, and when our easy road is lined with luxuriant flowers and fruit.

THE MIGHT OF FRAILTY

Psalm 105:23-36.

That is the wonder of wonders, That the Almighty God will use frail humility as vehicles of his power, and will make Moses and Aaron shine with reflected glory. Man can send an electric current into a fragile carbon film and make it incandescent. He can send his voice across continents, and make his picture or videos be seen in seconds anywhere in the world. And the Lord God can do wonders compared with which these are only as the dimmest dreams which man could imagine. He can send His holy power into human speech, and the words can wake the dead, he can send his Virtue into the human will, and its strength can shake thrones of iniquity, he can send His love into the human heart, and the power of its affection can capture the bitterest foe.

And so, the word "impossible" becomes itself impossible when the soul of man is in fellowship with the Lord of hosts. The pliant will becomes an iron pillar. The weak heart becomes "As a defended city" when it is the home of God. Dumb lips become the thrones of mysterious eloquence when touched with divine inspiration.

GRACE REIGNS

Romans 5:12-21.

When old Mr. Honest came to the river, and he entered the cold waters of death, the last words he was heard to utter by those who stood on the shore were these: "Grace reigns!" All through his pilgrimage old Mr. Honest had been in Emmanuel's land where grace reigned night and day. It was through grace that he had found the way of life. It was through grace that he had been delivered from the beasts and pitfalls of the road. It was grace that had given him lilies of peace, and springs of refreshment, and the fine air that inspired him in difficult tasks.

And unto death he still found "Grace abounding", and the Lord of the changing road was also Lord of the dark waters through which he passed into the radiant glories of the cloudless day.

In every yard of a faithful pilgrimage we shall find the decrees of sovereign love. We are never in alien country.

"Grace reigns" in every hill and valley, through every green pasture and over every rugged road, in every moment of "the day of life", and in the last sharp passage through the transient night of death.

BIBLE SCRIPTURE
SUDOKU

TAMPERING WITH THE LABEL

1 John 3:4-10.

Sin is transgression. It is the deliberate climbing of the fence. We see the trespassing placards, and in spite of the warning, we stride into the forbidden field. Sin is not ignorance, it is intention. We sin when we are wide awake! There are teachers abroad who would soften words like these. They offer terms which appear to lessen the harshness of our actions; they give our sin an aspect of innocence. But to alter the label on the bottle does not change the character of the contents. Poison is poison, give it what name you please. "Sin is the transgression of the law".

Let us be on guard against the men whose pockets are filled with deceptive labels. Let us vigilantly resist all teachings which would chloroform the conscience. Let us prefer true terms to merely nice ones. Let us call sin by its right name, and let us tolerate no moral conjuring either with ourselves or with others.

The first essential in all moral reformation is to call sin...sin. "If we confess our sin he is faithful and just to forgive us our sin".

MY INTERNAL THOUGHTS...

Psalm 89.

"Thou knowest my thought afar off!" That fills me with awe. I cannot find a hiding place where I can sun in secrecy. I cannot build an apparent sanctuary and conceal evil within its walls. I cannot with a sheep's skin hide the wolf. I cannot wrap up my jealousy in flattery and keep it unknown. "Thou God seest me". He knows the bottom thought that creeps in the basement of my being.

Nothing surprises God! He sees all my skin. So, I am filled with awe. "Thou knowest my thought afar off", filling me also with hope and joy. He sees the faintest, weakest desire, aspiring after goodness. He sees the smallest fire of affection burning uncertainly in my soul. He sees every moment of penitence which looks toward home. He sees every little triumph, and every altar I build along life's way. Nothing is overlooked.

My God is not a policeman, only looking for crimes; He is the God of grace, looking for graces, searching for jewels to adorn His crown. So I am filled with hope and joy.

THE SUBTLETY OF TEMPTATION

James 1:12-20.

Evil enticements always come to us in borrowed attire. In the olden days in a certain war...ammunition was carried out in piano cases, and military advices or secrets were transmitted in the skins of melons. And that is the way of the enemy of our souls. He makes us think we are receiving music when he is sending explosives; he promises...life, but his gift is laden with seeds of death. He offers us liberty, and he hides his chains in dazzling flowers. "Things are not...what they seem".

And so our enemy uses mirages, and will-o'-the-wisps and tinseled crowns. He lights friendly fires on perilous coasts to snare us to our ruins upon the rocks near the shore. And therefore we need clear and sure eyes. We need a refined moral compass with a sense that can discriminate between true and false, and which can discern the enemy even "when he comes as an angel of light". And we may have the wisdom. "By His grace we may be kept morally sensitive, and we shall know our foe even when he is a long way off thinking we do not see him through the fog when the Lord is our eyes through anything and any storm."

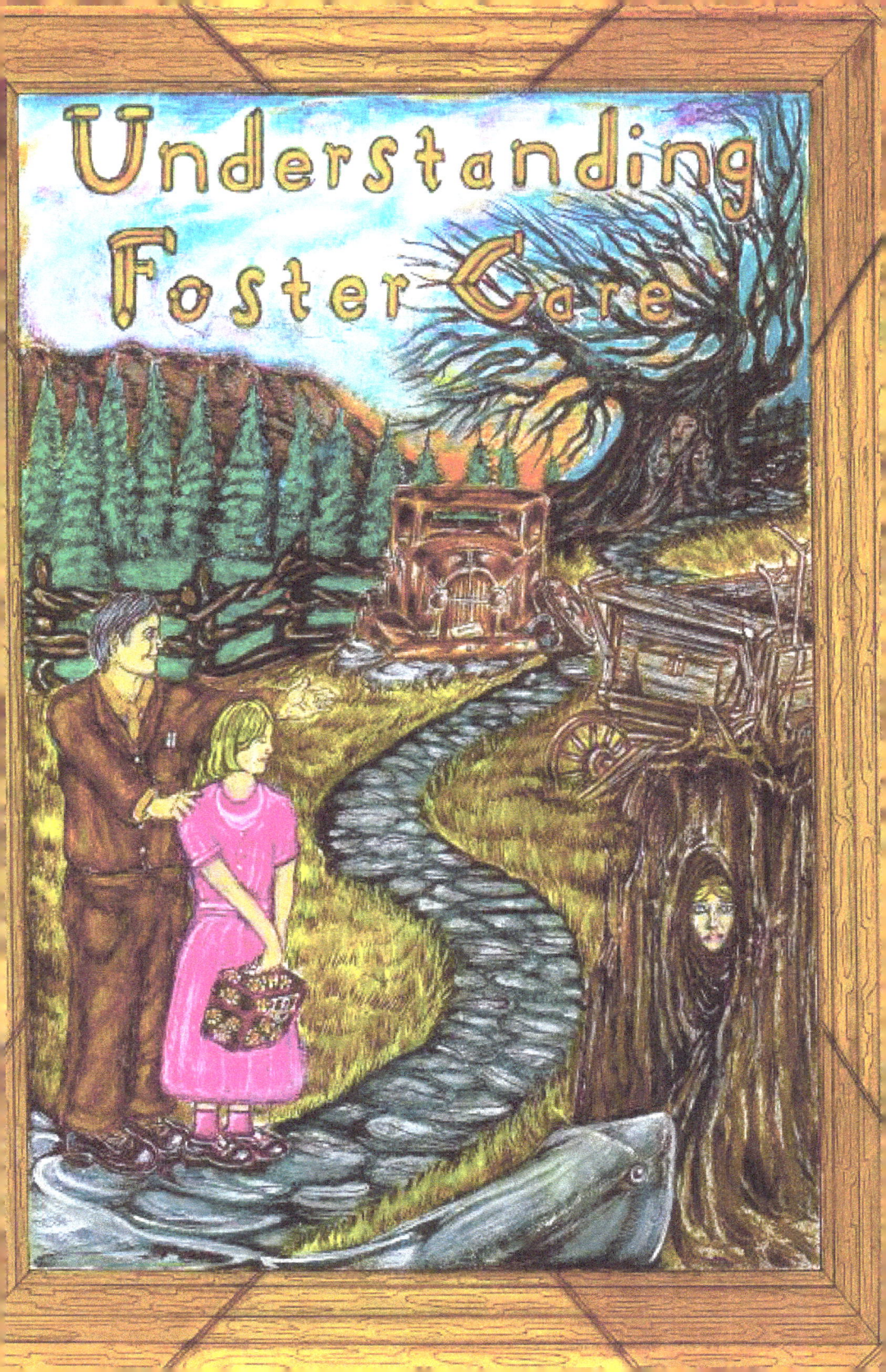

THE ROCK AND THE BOWING WALL

Psalm 62.

Here are two symbols by which the psalmist describes the confidence of righteousness. "He only is my rock". Many years ago I had a shelter of a great rock on a storm-swept mountain side. The wind tore along the heights, driving the rain like hail, but in the opening of the rock our shelter was complete.

And the second symbol is this; "He is my high place". The high place is the home of the chamois, out of reach of the arrow. "Flee as a bird to your mountain!" Get beyond the hunters' range! Our security is found in loftiness. It is our unutterable privilege to live in the heavenly places Christ Jesus is in. Such is the confidence of the righteous.

In the psalm there is also another pair of symbols describing the futility of the wicked. The wicked is "A Bowing wall". The wall is out of perpendicular, out of conformity with the truth of the plumb-line, and it will assuredly topple into ruin. So it is with the wicked: he is building awry, and he will fall into moral disaster. He is also "as a tottering fence." The wind and the rain dislodge the fence, it rots at its foundations, and one day it lies prone upon the ground.

REVISITING OLD ALTARS

"I will make there an altar unto God, Who answered me in the day
of my distress..."
Genesis 35:1-7

It is a blessing to revisit our early altars. It is a good thing to return to
the haunts of early vision. Places and things have their sanctifying
influences, and can recall us to lost experiences. I know a man to
whom the scent of a white and wild rose is always a call to prayer. I
know another to whom Grasmere is always the window of Holy
vision. Sometimes a particular pew in a particular Church can throw
the heavens open, and we see the Son of God. The old Sunday-
School has sometimes taken an old man back to his childhood and
brought him closer to God. So I do not wonder that God led Jacob
back to Bethel, and that in the old place of blessing he reconstructed
himself to the Lord.

It is a revelation of the loving-kindness of God that we have all these
helps to the recovery of past experiences. Let us use them with
reverence. And in our early days let us make them. Let us build altars
of communion which later in life we shall love to revisit. Let us make
early our home. "The house of God and the gate of heaven". Let us
multiply deeds of service which will make countless places fragrant
for all our after years.

THE VALUE OF THE SOUL

Matthew 18:7-14.

What an infinite value the Lord attaches to one soul! And one of them that has gone astray! I thought he might have missed the one! And yet the Eastern Shepherd says that out of his great flock he can miss the individual face. A face is missing, as though a child were absent from a family circle like our daughter, Holly. When a soul is wandering in the city or far country, there is an awful gap in the father's house! Is thy place empty? Is mine?

And mark the pangs of the shepherd's quest. "He goeth into the mountain and seeketh!" The eastern shepherd goes out in the tempest, and in rocky ravine and turmoiled weather or in thorny shrub that tears the hands and the feet, he or she seeks and finds his or her sheep. And my Lord sought me, in the darkness and in the stony and thorny places and in the awful desolations of the hills and valleys.

And the shepherd found his or her sheep, and he or she returns across the hills singing a song filled with triumph of grace...at seeing the shepherd's quarry again. Reunification with family always allows the father to rejoice.

FALSE SHEPHERDS

Ezekiel 34:1-10.

His word of the Lord puts before me the unlovingly lineaments of the false shepherds. They are self-seeking. "They feed themselves," but they "feed not the flock". They take up religion for what they can make out of it!

It is a carnal ambition, not a holy service. It is used for getting, not for giving, for self-gratification and self-glorification and not for self-sacrifice. It is selfishness masquerading as holiness, a thief in the garb of the shepherd.

And, therefore, the false shepherds are devoid of sympathy. "The diseased have ye not strengthened, neither have ye healed that which was sick." Selfishness always tends to benumbment. Humaneness is fostered by sacrifice. Our sympathetic chords are kept refined by chivalrous deeds. Drop the deeds and all our refinements begin to coarsen, and we make no response to our brother's or sister's cries of need and pain.

And because there is no sympathy there is no quest: "My Shepherd wandered... and none did seek after them". How can we seek them if we have never missed them, if we have no sense that they are lost? And, I must share if I would share in the search.

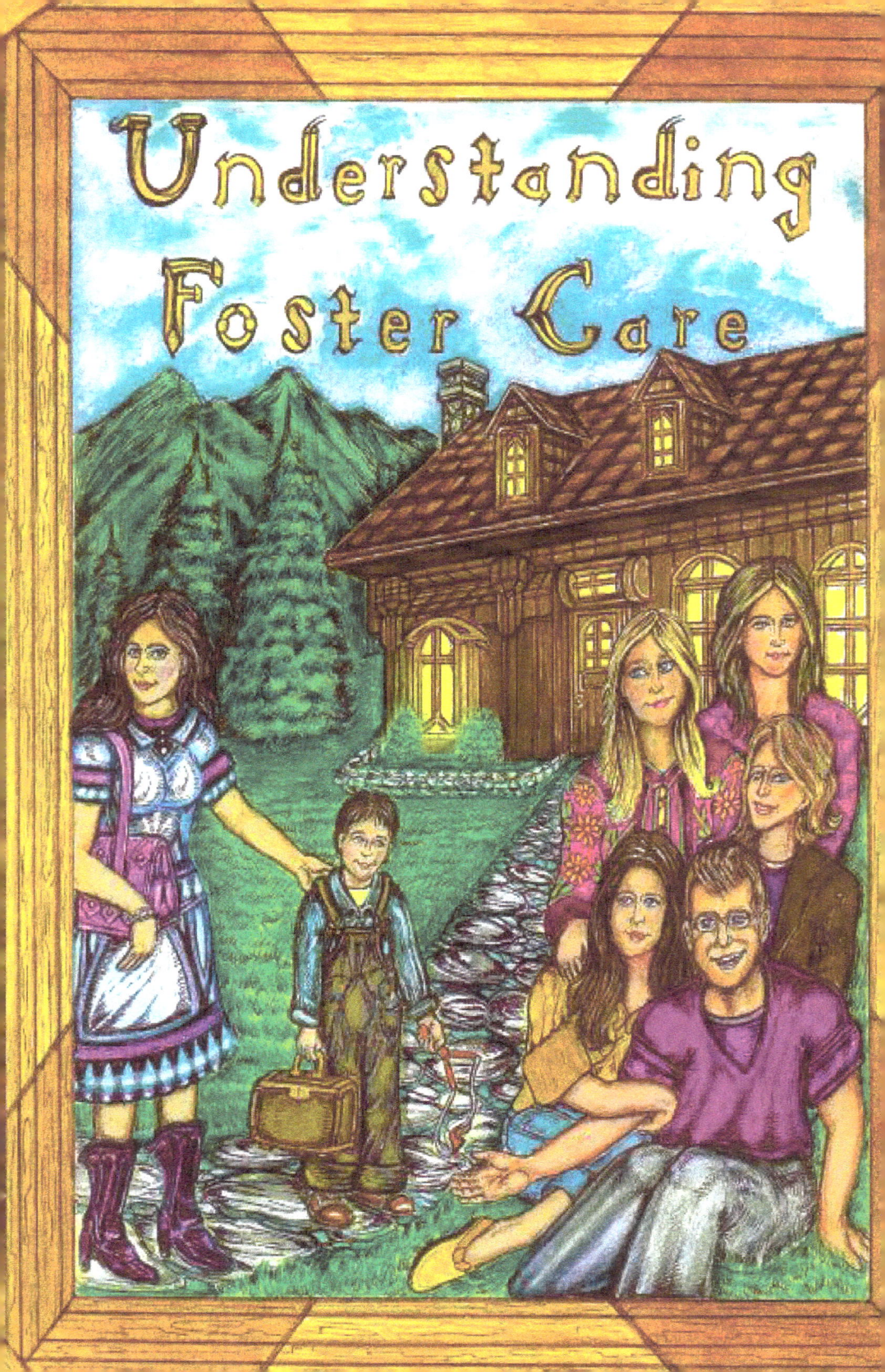

MY OWN SHEPHERD

Psalm 23.

With my wife's favorite Scripture, how do I touch this without bruising what is so lovely to Maralee? Like the Psalm, she is exquisite as a violet by a mossy stone! Exposition is almost an impertinence, its grace is so simple and winsome.

There is a ministry of rest. "He maketh me to lie down in green pastures". The good Shepherd knows when my spirit needs relaxation. He will not have me always "on the stretch". The bow of the best violin sometimes requires to have its strings "let down". And so our Lord gives us rest.

And there is the discipline of change. "He leadeth me in the paths of righteousness". Those strange roads in life, unknown roads by which we all pass into changed circumstances and surroundings! But discipline of the change is only to bring me into new pastures, that we may gain new fresh nutrients for our soul. "Because they have no changes they fear not God".

And there is "the valley of the shadow of death", cold and bare! What matter? He is there! "I will fear no evil". What if I see no "pastures green?" "Thy rod and thy staff they comfort me!" The Lord who is leading me, will see after my food. "Thou preparest a table before me in the presence of mine enemies". I have a quiet feast while my foes are looking on! Reliance on God's grace among the principalities of people, places and things outside and inside our families that try each of us. Reliance on the Good Shepherd.

DISCERNMENT

John 10:19-30.

His is Spiritual Discernment. We may test our growth in grace by our expertness in detecting the voice of our Lord. It is the skill of the saint to catch "the still small voice" amid all the selfish clamours of the day, and amid the far more subtle callings of the heart. It needs a good ear to catch the voice of the Lord in our sorrows. I think it requires a better ear to discern the voice amid our joys! The twilight helped me to be serious; the noonday glare tends to make me heedless "And they follow me". Discernment is succeeded by obedience. That is the one condition of becoming a saint—to follow the immediate call of the Lord. And it is the one condition of becoming an expert listener.

Every time I hear the voice and follow, I sharpen my sense of hearing, and the next time the voice will sound more clear.

"And I give unto them eternal life." Yes, life is found in the ways of a listening obedience. "Every faculty and function will be vitalized when I follow the Lord of life and glory." "In Christ shall be made alive".

My Savior, graciously give me the listening ear! Give me the obedient heart.

THE DISTINCTION OF BEING RECOGNIZED

John 10:01-18.

The Good Shepherd knows his or her sheep, and knows them by name. And that is what I am tempted to forget. I think about myself as one of the innumerable multitude, no one of whom receives personal attention. "My way is overlooked by my God." But here is the evangel—the Savior would miss me, even... me!

At a great orchestral rehearsal, which Sir Michael Costa was conducting, the man who played the piccolo stayed his fingers for a moment, thinking that his trifling contributions would never be missed. At once Sir Michael raised his hand and said, "Stop"! "Where's the piccolo?" "He missed the individual note." And my Lord needs the note of my life to make the music of his kingdom, and if the note be absent, he will miss it, and the glorious music will be broken and incomplete.

There is a common voice of self-conceit, but there is also a common voice of excessive self-depreciation. "My Lord can do nothing with me!" Yes, my Lord knows these and needs these! And by the power of his grace thou can accomplish wonders!

FORGETTING GOD

Deuteronomy 8:11-20.

"Beware...lest when thou hast eaten and art full...thine heart be lifted up, and thou forget the Lord thy God". I was in a little cabin once in Maine. I said to a friend who lived in it, "Can you see the Castle from here?" and he replied; "We can see it best in the winter when the leaves are off the trees." "In the summertime it is likely to be hid." The summer bounty hid the castle; the winter barrenness revealed it! And so, it is in life. In the season of fullness, we are prone to be blind to "the house of many mansions", and we forget the Master of our house, the Lord God, our material wealth hides our eternal treasure.

What then shall we do in the days of prosperity, when all our trees are in full leaf? We must pray that material things may never become opaque, that they may be always transparent, so that through the seen we may behold the unseen. This is a gift of the Spirit, and may be ours. He will anoint our eyes with the vision of grace, and everything will become to us a symbol of something better, so that even in the midst of material plenty our hearts will be with our treasure in heaven. Everything will be to us "as if it were transparent glass...clearly seen by grace...with our Lord God."

A MIRACLE IN A DRY PLACE

Psalm 107:33-43.

He Turneth... the dry ground into water-springs." This is one of the miracles of grace. The good Lord makes a dry experience the fountain of blessing. I pass into an apparently wasted place and I find riches of consolation. Even in "the Valley of the shadow" I come upon "green pastures" and "still waters". I find flowers in the ruts of the harvest roads if I am in the way of God's commandments. God's Providence is the pioneer of every faithful believer. "His blessed Feet have gone before". Whatever I will need is already foreseen, and foresight with the Lord means forethought and provision. Every hour gives the loyal disciples surprises of grace.

Let me therefore not fear when the path of duty turns into the wilderness. The wilderness is as habitable with God as the crowded city, and in His Fellowship my bread and water are sure. The Lord has strange manna for the children of disappointment, and he makes water "gush forth from the rock". Duty can lead me nowhere without Him, and His provision is abundant both in "the thirsty desert and the dewy mead." There will be a spring at the foot of every hill, and I shall find "lilies of peace" in the lonely valley of humiliation.

THE CONFESSION OF SIN

"I acknowledge my transgressions; and my sin is ever before me..."
Psalm 51:1-12

Sin that is unconfessed shuts out the energies of grace. Confession makes the soul receptive of the bountiful waters of life. We open the door to God as soon as we name our sin. Guilt that is penitently confessed is already in the "consuming fire" of God's love.

When I "acknowledge my sin" I begin to enter into the knowledge of "Pardon", joy, peace". But if I hide my sin I also hide myself from "The unsearchable riches of Christ." "If we confess our sins He is faithful and just to forgive us our sins and to cleanse us from all unrighteousness."

I must then make confession of sin to God in my daily exercises in the presence of Jesus and the Holy Spirit. I am taking the way to recovered victory when I tell the Lord the story of my defeat. Satan strengthens his awful chains when he can induce me to keep silence concerning my sin. All his plans are thrown into confusion as soon as I "pour out my soul before the Lord".

When I fall let me not add to my guilt the further sin of secrecy. Unconfessed sin breeds a lurking-place and multiplies its hateful offspring. The soul that makes confession is washed through and through, and the seeds of iniquity are driven out of our souls!

PART 3

LEAVING ITS MARK

"Fear not, Thou worm Jacob, I will make thee a threshing
instrument with teeth..."
Isaiah 41:8-14

Could any two things be in greater contrast than a worm and an
instrument with teeth? The worm is delicate, bruised by a stone,
crushed beneath a passing wheel; an instrument with teeth can break
and not be broken, it can give its mark upon the rock.

And the mighty God can convert the one into the other. He can take
a man or a nation, who has all the impotence of the worm, and by the
invigoration of His own Spirit He can endow them with strength by
which they will leave a noble mark upon the history of their time.

And so, the worm may take heart. The Mighty God can make us
stronger than our circumstances. We can bend them all to our good.
In God's strength we can make them all pay tribute to our souls. We
can even take hold of a black disappointment, break it open, and
extract some jewel of grace. When God gives us wills like iron we can
drive through difficulties as the iron share cuts through the toughest
soil. "I will make thee," saith the Lord, "and shall he not do it?"

THE GIVER'S HAND

Genesis 4:3-15.

Cain and Abel both brought an offering unto the Lord, but one was accepted and the other was rejected. It is the giver who determines the worth or the worthlessness of the gift. God looks not at the gift, but at the hands that bring it. "Your hands are full of blood"! "Your hands are unclean!" The Lord demands "clean hands". He will not have our compliments if there is defilement behind them. Our courtesies are rejected if iniquity attends them. The shining gloss on the linen is an offense if the dirt is visible! Who cares for food presented by unclean hands? "Be ye clean, ye that bear the vessels of the Lord!"

Every gift is welcome to the Lord if offered with clean hands. A mite, or a cup of cold water, or our daily labour, or the first-fruits of a garden or field—all receive the blessings of our God if the hands that bring them are free from defilement. So is it with everything we offer to the Lord.

A song of praise makes sweet music in the hearing of our God if it comes from pure lips. Quoting God's scripture or promises as leading grace within a world of sinfulness needs to be foundational in true purity by a believer. Purity, as Thomas à Kempis says: "give the wings which carry everything into the Father's presence".

FIRST, MY BROTHER OR SISTER!

Matthew 10:17-24

"First be reconciled to the Brother or Sister." We are to put first things first. When we bring a gift unto the Lord he looks at the hand that brings it. If the hand is defiled the gift is rejected. "Wash you, make yourself clean." "First be reconciled to thy Brother or Sister, and then come and offer thy gift."

All this tells us why some resplendent gifts are rejected, and why some commonplace gifts are received amid heavenly song. This is why the widow's mite goes shining through the years. The hand that offered it was hallowed and purified with sacrifice. Shall we say that in that palm there is something akin to the pierced hands of the Lord? The mite had intimate associations with the cross.

And it also tells me why so much of our public worship is offensive to the Lord. We come to the church from a broken friendship. Some holy thing has been broken on the way. Someone's estate has been violated or invaded, and his or her treasures spoiled. Someone has been wronged, and God will not touch the gift. "Leave there thy gift; first be reconciled to thy Brother & Sister."

THE FIRE OF ENVY

James 3:13-18

In modern life, there are mixtures of alcohol and drug combinations and pills that have the power to pervert the senses of anyone who ingests them. Nothing is apprehended truly. Sight & hearing and taste are all distorted, and the victim is all unconscious of the confusion. The deadly potions are the minister of chaos. Envy is like those potions... when it is drunk by the spirit. It perverts every moral and spiritual sense. The envious is more fatally stricken than the blind. He or she gazes upon untruth and thinks it's true. He or she looks upon confusion and thinks it is order. Envy is color blind. It is like jealousy, of which it is a blood relation. It never sees anything in its natural hues. It misinterprets everything.

No one can quench the unholy fire of envy but the Mighty God Himself. It is like a prairie fire: Once kindled it is beyond our power to stamp it out. But, God's coolness is more than a match for our feverish heat.

His quenchings are transformations. He converts the perverted and changes envy into goodwill. The bitter pool is made sweet. For confusion, He gives order, for ashes He gives beauty, and in the face of an old enemy, we see the countenance of a friend. "Where envying and strife is, there is confusion & every evil work"!

NOBLE REVENGE

"I have delivered him that without cause is mine enemy".
Psalm 7:4

That is the noblest revenge, and in those moments David had intimate knowledge of the spirit of his Lord. "If thine enemy, feed him!"

Evil for good is Devil like. To receive a favor and to return a blow! To obtain the gift of language, and then to use one's speech to curse the giver! To use a sacred sword is unholy warfare! All this: Devil like. Evil for Evil is beast like. Yes, the bites back when it is bitten. The dog returns snarl for snarl, Venom for venom. And if, when I have been injured, I "pay a man back in his own coins", if I "give him as good as he gave", I am living on the plane of the beast.

Good for good is man-like. When I requite a man's kindness by kindness! When I send presents to one who loads me with benefits! This is a true and manly thing to do, and lifts us far above the beast.

Good for evil is god-like. Yes, that lifts me into "the heavenly places in Jesus Christ." The I have "The mind of Christ." Then do I do unto others as my Saviour has done unto me.

As you therefore have received Christ Jesus the Lord, so walk in Him

Colossians 2:6

SCRIPTURE REFERENCES FROM THE KING JAMES BIBLE

John 11:1-16

Psalm 119:33-40

John 18:1-14

John 18:15-27

Luke 17:22-32

2 Corinthians 6:11-18

2 Timothy 4:1-8

John 21:1-7

John 17:20-26

John 14:15-31

John 10:11-18

Luke 21:25-36

Hebrews 11:17-22

Deuteronomy 8:1-10

Psalm 105:23-36

Romans 5:12-21

1 John 3:4-10

Psalm 89

James 1:12-20

Psalm 62

Genesis 35:1-7

Matthew 18:7-14

Ezekiel 34:1-10

Psalm 23

John 10:19-30

John 10:1-18

Deuteronomy 8:11-20

Psalm 107:33-43

Psalm 51:1-12

Isaiah 41:8-14

Genesis 4:3-15

Matthew 10:17-24

James 3:13-18

Psalm 7:4

Psalm 57

Psalm 142

Matthew 10:16-28

Psalm 114

Isaiah 43:1-7

Psalm 91

Hebrews 11:1-7

Ephesians 4:25-32

Psalm 78:1-8

Psalm 34:9-22

James 5:7-11

Revelation 22:1-14

Deuteronomy 4:5-13

John 19:23-27

Joshua 8:30-35

Joshua 24:22-28

John 14:15-24

Leviticus 19:11-18

www.ingramcontent.com/pod-product-compliance
Lightning Source LLC
Chambersburg PA
CBHW051642120626
46551CB00014B/2182